Date: 10/7/21

J BIO MAYFIELD
Fishman, Jon M.,
Baker Mayfield /

SPORTS
ALL-STARS

BAKER MAYFIELD

Jon M. Fishman

Lerner Publications ◆ Minneapolis

Lerner Publications Company
An imprint of Lerner Publishing Group, Inc.
241 First Avenue North
Minneapolis, MN 55401 USA

For reading levels and more information, look up this title at www.lernerbooks.com.

Main body text set in Albany Std 22. Typeface provided by Agfa.

Editor: Rebecca Higgins **Photo Editor:** Brianna Kaiser

Library of Congress Cataloging-in-Publication Data

Names: Fishman, Jon M., author.
Title: Baker Mayfield / Jon M. Fishman.
Description: Minneapolis : Lerner Publications, [2021] | Series: Sports all-stars (Lerner sports) | Includes bibliographical references and index. | Audience: Ages 7–11 | Audience: Grades 2–3 | Summary: "Cleveland Browns quarterback Baker Mayfield is a Heisman winner and the 2018 first overall draft pick. As a rookie, he proved himself with an amazing comeback in his first NFL game. Read his story!"— Provided by publisher.
Identifiers: LCCN 2019057293 (print) | LCCN 2019057294 (ebook) | ISBN 9781541597488 (library binding) | ISBN 9781728414003 (paperback) | ISBN 9781728400976 (ebook)
Subjects: LCSH: Mayfield, Baker, 1995– —Juvenile literature. | Football players—United States—Biography—Juvenile literature. | Quarterbacks (Football)—United States—Biography. | Cleveland Browns (Football team : 1999-)—History.
Classification: LCC GV939.M2972 F57 2021 (print) | LCC GV939.M2972 (ebook) | DDC 796.332092 [B]—dc23

LC record available at https://lccn.loc.gov/2019057293
LC ebook record available at https://lccn.loc.gov/2019057294

Manufactured in the United States of America
1-47852-48292-4/6/2020

CONTENTS

In the Hunt 4

Facts at a Glance 5

Sports Fan 8

"Burning Desire" 13

Popular Player 18

Winning the Future 24

All-Star Stats 28

Glossary 29

Source Notes 30

Further Information 31

Index 32

Baker Mayfield passes the ball in 2019.

The 2019 Cleveland Browns were supposed to be good. The season before, they won five of seven games to end the year. In the **off-season**, superstar Odell Beckham Jr. joined the team.

- **Date of birth:** April 14, 1995

- **Position:** quarterback

- **League:** National Football League (NFL)

- **Professional highlights:** chosen with the first pick in the 2018 NFL Draft; helped Cleveland win seven games in 2018; threw 27 touchdown passes as a rookie, an all-time record for a first-year player

- **Personal highlights:** grew up in Austin, Texas; loves to play *Halo*; won the 2017 **Heisman Trophy**

Cleveland's quarterback, Baker Mayfield, was one of the hottest stars in the NFL. But after eight games in 2019, the Browns had a terrible 2–6 record.

Then they started to win. They beat the Buffalo Bills by three points. They topped the Pittsburgh Steelers by two touchdowns. On November 24, they faced the Miami Dolphins in Cleveland.

The Browns started the game with the ball. Mayfield led his team 68 yards down the field. Then he threw a 7-yard pass to Jarvis Landry for the first touchdown of the game. But Mayfield wasn't satisfied with a one-touchdown lead.

Mayfield has a strong throwing arm.

Mayfield dodges Dolphins defenders.

Later in the first quarter, Mayfield scanned the field for an open teammate. He sidestepped a charging Miami defender and heaved the ball. It soared 35 yards to the end zone and into the hands of Beckham Jr. Touchdown!

By halftime, the Browns were ahead 28–3. Miami played better in the second half, but they couldn't catch up. Cleveland won 41–24.

Mayfield threw three touchdown passes in the game, the most he'd thrown that season. More important, the win gave Cleveland a 5–6 record. They were ready to compete for a place in the playoffs.

Mayfield looks for an open teammate in 2019.

Baker Reagan Mayfield was born in Austin, Texas, on April 14, 1995. He grew up in Austin with his brother, Matt, and their parents, Gina and James Mayfield. Matt is about five years older than Baker.

Baker's first name was inspired by Baker Montgomery, one of James's high school football teammates. Baker's middle name honors Ronald Reagan, the 40th president of the United States.

Baker has loved sports for as long as he can remember. One day when he was three, he was watching cartoons on TV with his mother. He told her that from now on, he wanted to watch only sports on TV. Then he changed the channel to ESPN.

No matter what game Baker played, he wanted

Reagan served as president from 1981–1989.

Baker's love of football started when he was a kid.

to win. He played checkers, Ping-Pong, and hide-and-seek with his family. In the summer, he called friends to organize football and baseball games in his yard. His mother said Baker's summers consisted of three main activities. "Baseball, football, jump in the pool," Gina said.

Baker played baseball and football at Lake Travis High School. In 2009, the freshman stood 5 feet 2 inches (1.6 m) tall. But by his junior year, he was 5 feet 10 inches (1.8 m) and ready to take over as the **varsity** quarterback.

That season Baker threw 45 touchdown passes and just five **interceptions**. He led Lake Travis to victory in the 2011 Texas state championship. As a senior in 2012, he threw 22 touchdowns and three interceptions.

Baker's amazing high school stats should have attracted interest from the biggest college football teams in the United States. But some coaches thought he wasn't big enough to play quarterback at the college level. They believed his hands were too small to get a strong grip on the ball. They said he didn't run fast enough.

Recruiters judged Baker because of his size.

Texas Tech plays at Jones AT&T Stadium.

Colleges in Washington, New Mexico, and Florida offered Baker **scholarships**. But he wanted to attend a school that had a more successful football team. In 2013, he enrolled at Texas Tech and tried out for the team. He made it and became the starting quarterback. He was the first freshman **walk-on** at a top college to ever start the season as the team's quarterback.

In 2015, Mayfield joined the University of Oklahoma football team.

Mayfield threw 12 touchdown passes in his first season with Texas Tech. He won an award naming him the best freshman offensive player in his **conference**. But he didn't get along with the team's head coach. Mayfield left Texas Tech after one season.

In 2015, Mayfield enrolled at the University of Oklahoma. Just as he had at Texas Tech, Mayfield joined the school's football team as a walk-on. Then he took over as Oklahoma's starting quarterback.

Mayfield played three incredible years at Oklahoma. He averaged almost 40 touchdown passes per season. He won many awards, including the 2017 Heisman Trophy. In 2018, the Browns chose Mayfield with the first overall pick in the NFL Draft.

Mayfield poses with the 2017 Heisman Trophy.

Mayfield worked hard to prove himself in Cleveland.

Hue Jackson was Cleveland's head coach that year. "[Mayfield] has a burning desire to be the best," Jackson said. The day after the draft, the young quarterback proved his coach right. Instead of celebrating, he went to the gym to work out.

During the season, an NFL player's days are filled with practices, meetings, and games. Tuesday is usually the only day of the week players have to themselves. But during the off-season, Mayfield sets his own schedule. He stays in shape with tough workouts.

Mayfield practices throwing in 2018.

Mayfield starts each day with coffee and a shower followed by breakfast. In college, he ate a lot of breakfast tacos, burgers, and other high-calorie foods. As an NFL player, he fuels his workouts with egg whites, turkey, and vegetables.

Mayfield often exercises with his brother. Together, they do push-ups, pull-ups, and other common moves.

But the brothers also try out new ways to stay fit. They race each other through a grid on the ground, stepping from one space to the next as quickly as they can. In one **drill**, Mayfield does a push-up, throws a heavy exercise ball, and then takes off running. He knows it's important to make workouts fun.

Mayfield and Beckham Jr. warm up together before a game.

Mayfield's brother isn't his only off-season workout partner. He has exercised with teammate Odell Beckham Jr., Milwaukee Brewers outfielder Christian Yelich, and actor Mark Wahlberg.

POPULAR
PLAYER

Fans love watching
Mayfield play.

At the University of Oklahoma, Mayfield became a national superstar.
Just ask families that had babies in 2017. That year Baker was one of the fastest-growing names for babies born in the United States.

Mayfield and his wife, Emily, attend a sports dinner in 2018.

Mayfield's popularity carried over to the NFL. In 2018, sales of his Cleveland jersey ranked second in the league. Fans loved Mayfield, and companies noticed. He signed deals to **endorse** sports gear, drinks, and headphones. In 2019, Mayfield began appearing in TV commercials with his wife, Emily Mayfield. The fun ads pretended the couple lived at Cleveland's football stadium.

Halo

In high school, Mayfield fell in love with the video game *Halo*. As he did with all games, he played to win. He practiced for hours every day. He decided to become a pro gamer and compete in *Halo* tournaments for money.

Luckily for Browns fans, Mayfield changed his mind and focused on football instead of pro gaming. But he hasn't given up playing *Halo* for fun. Mayfield even credits video games with helping him think and react more quickly on the field.

Mayfield plays in a 2018 gaming tournament.

Mayfield practices batting with the Milwaukee Brewers.

Though Mayfield's football career took off, he never lost his love for baseball. In March 2019, Mayfield attended a spring training game with Yelich and the Brewers. The quarterback hit balls during pregame batting practice. Then he spent three innings as Milwaukee's first base coach.

Mayfield leaps to reach home plate in a charity baseball game.

Mayfield has fun with his fame and success. He also helps people in the Cleveland area by raising money for Special Olympics and other groups. At a charity **auction** in 2018, people bid on prizes such as dinner with the Mayfields. The couple helped raise more than $110,000 in 10 minutes for housing for kids. "Absolutely unbelievable," Mayfield wrote on Twitter.

Mayfield's longest completed throw was 89 yards.

The Browns lose to the Pittsburgh Steelers in 2017.

The Browns were desperate in 2018.

The NFL Draft order is ranked by the previous year's team records. The team with the worst record picks first, and the team that won the Super Bowl picks last. Cleveland had the top pick in the draft because they hadn't won any games in 2017. The Browns hadn't had a winning season in 10 years.

When Mayfield joined Cleveland in 2018, he became a source of hope for the team and its fans. As a two-time college walk-on who became the NFL's top draft pick, he had proved he was a special player. Maybe he was special enough to lead the Browns to the playoffs.

Cleveland's 2018 season began like many recent seasons. After nine games, the Browns had an ugly 2–6–1 record. But as Mayfield became more comfortable in the NFL, the team played better. In game 10

Mayfield threw 22 touchdowns in 2019.

Mayfield (*left*) and teammates celebrate after a touchdown in 2018.

against the Atlanta Falcons, he threw three touchdown passes to win. He threw four scoring passes the next week to help the Browns beat the Cincinnati Bengals. The team's defense played better too, holding most opponents to 20 points or fewer. The Browns finished the year 7–8–1.

In 2019, hopes were high in Cleveland. But once again, the Browns fell out of the playoff chase early in the season and couldn't recover. Mayfield knows he will be judged by his team's success in the NFL, not by what he did in college. "You have to hit the reset button," he said. "What I've done in the past doesn't matter." For Mayfield and the Browns, the future is looking much brighter than the past.

Mayfield looks forward to more success on the field.

All-Star Stats

New York Giants running back Saquon Barkley won the 2018 NFL Offensive Rookie of the Year award. But many people thought the prize should have gone to Mayfield. He had one of the best seasons for a rookie quarterback in league history.

Most Touchdown Passes by a Rookie in NFL History

Player	Touchdown Passes	Year
Baker Mayfield	27	2018
Peyton Manning	26	1998
Russell Wilson	26	2012
Andrew Luck	23	2012
Dak Prescott	23	2016
Jim Kelly	22	1986
Butch Songin	22	1960
Jameis Winston	22	2015
Derek Carr	21	2014
Cam Newton	21	2011

Glossary

auction: a sale of something to the highest bidder

conference: a group of teams that play against one another

drill: an exercise designed to improve a skill

endorse: to recommend a product or service, usually in exchange for money

Heisman Trophy: an annual award given to college football's most outstanding player

interceptions: passes caught by the opposing team that result in a change of possession

off-season: the part of a year when a sports league is inactive

scholarships: money to help students pay for school

varsity: the top team at a school

walk-on: a college athlete who tries out for an athletic team without having been recruited or offered a scholarship

Source Notes

10 Tim Keown, "All He Needs Is Hate," ESPN, August 15, 2016, http://www.espn.com/espn/feature/story/_/id/17284078 /oklahoma-sooners-qb-baker-mayfield-used-defying-critics.

15 Mary Kay Cabot, "Browns Draft Baker Mayfield No. 1 Overall in 2018 NFL Draft," Cleveland.com, last modified April 27, 2018, https://www.cleveland.com/browns/2018/04 /browns_draft_baker_mayfield_no.html.

22 Courtney Shaw, "Baker Mayfield, Cleveland Quarterback, Helps Charity Raise $110k in 10 Minutes," NBC26, December 12, 2018, https://www.nbc26.com/sports/baker -mayfield-cleveland-quarterback-helps-charity-raise-110k -in-10-minutes.

27 Bill Bender, "Baker Mayfield's Connection to Cleveland Grows Heading into Exciting Offseason," Sporting News Australia, February 2, 2019, https://www.sportingnews .com/au/nfl/news/baker-mayfield-cleveland-browns-2019 -offseason-afc-playoff-contenders/17o144s0hcftp1v9yn gkwvq9a2.

Baker Mayfield
https://bakermayfield.com

Cleveland Browns
https://www.clevelandbrowns.com/

Coleman, Ted. *Baker Mayfield: Football Superstar.* Mendota Heights, MN: Press Room Editions, 2019.

Fishman, Jon M. *Christian Yelich.* Minneapolis: Lerner Publications, 2020.

Pro Football: Baker Mayfield
https://www.pro-football-reference.com/players/M/MayfBa00.htm

Whiting, Jim. *Cleveland Browns.* Mankato, MN: Creative Education, 2019.

Index

Cleveland Browns, 4–7, 14, 19–20, 24–27

ESPN, 9

Halo, 5, 20

interception, 11

Lake Travis High School, 10–11

NFL Draft, 5, 14–15, 24–25

Special Olympics, 22

Texas Tech, 12–14

touchdown, 5, 11, 13–14

Yelich, Christian, 17, 21

Photo Acknowledgments

Image credits: Jason Miller/Getty Images, p. 4; Kirk Irwin/Getty Images, pp. 6, 17, 27; Nick Cammett/Diamond Images/Getty Images, pp. 7, 15, 24, 25, 26; Jamie Sabau/Getty Images, p. 8; mark reinstein/Shutterstock.com, p. 9; JoeSAPhotos/Shutterstock.com, p. 10; wavebreakmedia/Shutterstock.com, p. 11; John E. Moore III/Getty Images, p. 12; Ronald Martinez/Getty Images, p. 13; Jeff Zelevansky/Getty Images, p. 14; Frank Jansky/Icon Sportswire/Getty Images, p. 16; Joe Robbins/Getty Images, p. 18; Matt Winkelmeyer/Getty Images, p. 19; Jerritt Clark/Getty Images, p. 20; Will Powers/Icon Sportswire/Getty Images, p. 21; Rich Polk/Getty Images, p. 22; Justin Edmonds/Getty Images, p. 23.

Cover: Ric Tapia/Icon Sportswire/Getty Images.